ANSWERING MY CALLING--

"AN INSPIRATIONAL GUIDE TO FULFILLING YOUR PURPOSE"

By: Winston Taylor, MSW

To order additional copies of this book, contact:
Xlibris Corporation
1-888-795-4274
www.Xlibris.com
Orders@Xlibris.com

DEDICATION

To my beloved mother, Doris E. Taylor, our sister Lenda Taylor, and our aunt Odessa T. Cooper, all of whom passed away too soon and are deeply missed. This book is also dedicated to my family, the Taylors, Coopers, Duboses, and Joneses. I also dedicate this book to the millions incarcerated in jails and prisons and those precious children and youth in foster care. Special thanks to Michelle R. Dunlap, PhD, who read my manuscript and gave me some helpful pointers.

CONTENTS

INTRODUCTION

For we are God's masterpiece. He has created us anew in Christ Jesus, so that we can do the good things he planned for us long ago. (Eph. 2:10, NLT)

Therefore I, a prisoner for serving the Lord, beg you to lead a life worthy of your calling, for you have been called by God. (Eph. 4:1, NLT)

This book was written to celebrate the human experience, to inspire anyone who is seeking a higher calling in his or her life to make a difference in his or her family and community, as well as worldwide.

The word "calling" throughout this book is referring to the service or ministry that God has called you to do. Whether spiritual work like a preacher of the Gospel, a deacon in your church, a person of faith in his or her daily setting in life or whether as the chief executive officer of the company or the janitor and all who are in between working a nine-to-five job and those who own their businesses, all have a calling(s). The word "calling" can also refer to a profession or vocation, such as a doctor, lawyer, social worker, counselor, singer, teacher, etc. The majority of us are a part of what is referred to as the laity or laypersons, which refers to the body of believers who are not the clergy (ordained preachers, ministers, pastors, bishops, etc.). In other words, the laity includes everyone else in the church (the choir, ushers, regular churchgoers, etc.). "Calling" and "purpose" are often used interchangeably by this author in this book.

I believe for such a time as this God is calling laypeople from all walks of life to become equipped, trained, and involved in service and volunteerism. Not one group of people, ordained or the laity, could possibly meet all the needs of the people in our world. Yes, the states, cities, towns, and federal governments as well as people of faith play key roles; however, they alone cannot address and combat all of the ills and problems (such as high incarceration rates especially for those of color, poverty, substance abuse, child abuse, mental health and physical health issues, affordable health care and housing, high school dropout rates, high college tuition costs, environmental concerns, infant mortality, high unemployment, homelessness, single-parent households, discrimination, racism, etc.) in our society. It will take all of us and community partnerships to restore families and communities.

The word "ministry" refers to service to those in need from a spiritual (godly) or secular (worldly) point of view. For example, you can provide ministry to the homeless by feeding them food, providing temporary shelter, and clothing them as well as teaching them about the *Lord*. You can also from a secular point of view train and teach those same homeless people mentioned earlier how to get their GEDs, attend college, gain job skills, get jobs, take care of their families, and live in their own homes, etc. No matter which route you take, spiritual or secular, you are still providing ministry or service to those in need. This author often uses the words "ministry" and "service" interchangeably in this book.

What or who inspires you? What do you enjoy doing the most? Whom can you depend on to help you realize your dreams and calling? Hopefully, this book can help you get started on your journey.

As you read the pages and complete the exercises in this book, I hope you will be inspired to roll up your sleeves, put on your thinking cap of possibilities, and allow the creative side of your mind to help you begin to chip away at any mountain of doubt, despair, and negativity you might have faced so you can be free in order to fulfill your purpose.

Chapter One

Purpose

> And we know that God causes everything to work together for the good of those who love God
> and are called according to his purpose for them. (Rom. 8:28, NLT)

When you go to bed each night, have you fulfilled your purpose that day? Do you feel good about what you are doing in your life right now? If you answered no to any of the above-mentioned questions, then you have the power to change your course and direction in life.

It will have to start with you and the way you look at things in life. Sometimes we can be our worst enemies and worst critics: *I can't go to college because I am not smart enough, I can't get the job promotion because I don't have . . .* "You can do all things through God that strengthens you" (Phil. 4:13 NLT).

You sure can make a difference and help make our world a better place in which to live by acting today. Yes, Jesus Christ is standing at the door and knocking on your heart to make a difference right in your own setting in life. You can play a vital role here on our planet Earth. No one else can share the particular gifts and talents that you were born to share with the world.

I believe many religious houses of faith from all denominations and beliefs equip and train the laity poorly, value their gifts poorly and underutilize them. Some of this is due to ignorance concerning the role and responsibilities of God's people, and some of it is due to selfishness and ungodliness on the part of some religious leaders.

When you believe in yourself and can visualize yourself overcoming all of the "isms" that have negatively impacted you in life, you will be taking the first steps to fulfilling your purpose. Each step afterward will become easier, and you will be moving closer toward achieving your goals in life.

Chapter Two

Excuses

Then you will know the truth, and the truth will set you free. (John 8:32, NIV)

When you have evaluated your situation in life, you can either take ownership, grow from experience(s), and move on to greater things, or you can give excuses why you are not where you need to be today. In fact, some people live out their entire lives blaming others for their plight in life. Don't get me wrong. We are all affected by someone else whether from childhood experiences all the way through adulthood experiences in various types of relationships and situations. That person may have set you back because you did not get the job promotion, or someone cheated on you in the relationship, just to name a few things. The point is these situations are painful, and it may take some time to heal, but you can still rise up and move beyond such hurts and letdowns. Excuses can be transformed into declarations of independency and "I cans." One of my favorite Bible verses is from Philippians 4:13 (NLT), "For I can do everything with the help of Christ who gives me the strength I need."

I believe what the Bible says, that "all things work together for the good" (Rom. 8:28, NLT). It is their loss and your gain. Thank God you survived that experience; perhaps it will make you stronger and may be the genesis of you fulfilling your purpose in life. Just say for example, if you have been in a domestic violence situation, now you may be able to be an advocate for others who are still trapped in domestic violence. You may be fortunate to do some volunteer hours or full-time work in a domestic violence shelter where you can help, encourage, and motivate other victims as well as educate and help treat the perpetrators.

There are countless people who are demonstrating each day that they are not allowing their victimization keep its ugly gripe on their lives. In fact, they are facing their abuse and abusers, addiction, low self-esteem, depression, guilt, etc., head-on so they can move forward and help others facing similar situations.

Chapter Three

Forgiving

> Be kind and compassionate to one another, forgiving each other, just as in Christ God forgave you. (Eph. 4:32, NIV)

Have you forgiven yourself for the hurts and pains you caused yourself and others? Nobody is perfect, and we all make mistakes in life, while some are more costly than others. In order to move on and become free, you must be able to tell yourself *I am sorry* and *I forgive myself.*

After you have forgiven yourself, with the help of the *Lord*, you can now move on toward forgiving others who have hurt and misused you. You may not forget all that you have done or all that was done against you, but you can have peace within yourself knowing that you have done your part in making things right. If the person you have asked forgiveness does not accept your sincere apology, then it is on him or her. You have done your part, and hopefully, that person will experience his or her own healing and accept your forgiveness in his or her own time.

When you have forgiven yourself and others and asked God to forgive you, I believe you are now ready to move on to the next dimension on your journey to fullness and wholeness.

Chapter Four

Healing

A time to kill and a time to heal, a time to tear down and a time to build. (Eccles. 3:3, NIV)

It may take you some time to heal from negative experiences in your life; and you should allow time for healing, reflecting, and refreshing. Healing is a natural process in life, and I often think about and compare it to how the seasons change. In the fall, the leaves have beautiful colors and finally wither away and fall off the trees. Come springtime, there is new growth and shoots come out, and the cycle repeats itself. During the winter, some of the weak, diseased tree limbs are broken by the winter storms. By summertime, the tree is providing shade, shelter, and food to many creatures and displaying its beauty as God's handiwork as it is growing all year-round. Broken limbs are replaced and rejuvenated, and the trees are able to bear much fruit each season.

People heal themselves in various ways. Some may choose traditional therapy while others may join some activity that helps repair the mind, body, and soul. Reading a good book like this one, attending a religious service or retreat, pursuing your hobbies, joining a social club or joining a gym, changing a job, moving to another location, taking a well-deserved vacation are examples of things one can do in order to begin the process of healing one's self of emotional and psychological hurts as well as physical fatigue.

You only know what is best for you in terms of the methods and means and the time frame for your healing. Listen to yourself and take care of yourself.

Chapter Five

Networking

Now all of you together are Christ's body, and each one of you is a separate and necessary part of it. (1 Cor. 12:27, NLT)

Networking is another powerful key to fulfilling your purpose and dreams. There is a saying that it is not what you know but who you know. **Making connections with like and different minds will make you stronger, as well as those whom you are networking with to achieve your goals.**

It is okay to move out of your comfort zones and learn something new, which will involve changing one's course and building new alliances. Whom do you need to join or make a part of your inner circle? With modern-day technology, you can network with partners all across this world, and nothing can stop you from living out your goals.

If you happen to be unemployed at this moment in your life and seeking employment or a career change, the best place to start is with family and friends who are working or in the career you are seeking. They know from inside of the company you're aiming to join if there are job openings or if there will be future positions available. Belonging to a social club or religious organization are also great places to network, just to name a few.

Chapter Six

Diligence

But without faith it is impossible to please him: for he that cometh to God must believe that he is, and that he is a rewarder of them that diligently seek him. (Heb. 11:6, KJV)

You should be diligent at whatever you set your mind to achieve. It may take one month or less or many years before you can realize a particular goal you have set for yourself, but don't let the time it takes for you to fulfill it be a hindrance. Enjoy the journey each step you take and celebrate each milestone you accomplish. **Work on your plan each day in season and out of season, and not for long you will see your dreams begin to take shape and take a life of its own.**

Diligence means if you have to get up early in the morning each day and hit the pavement running before the rush hour traffic in order to find that job or start that business or ministry or whatever you are trying to do, be persistent, consistent, and committed to it. Develop a plan and a method of how you will be implementing your plans. Yes, count the cost too. Put all you have in making your goals become realities!

Chapter Seven

Waiting

> Be still before the LORD and wait patiently for him; do not fret when men succeed in their ways,
> when they carry out their wicked schemes. (Ps. 37:7, NIV)

We live in a society today whereby everything is rush, rush: *I need it today. Hurry up. Give it to me now*. Modern technologies have helped us to access information all around the world with just one touch of a keyboard or an electronic device.

When I was a child, the time seemed so long, and I could not wait until summer vacations and all of the holidays to come. I am also an amateur artist, and I still struggle with trying to rush and complete an entire drawing or painting at just one sitting. I am learning that waiting is a key ingredient in life; and as one waits, he or she is not merely sitting in a corner twiddling his or her thumbs but is planning things out in one's life, making preparations for one's career, family, retirement, ministry, etc.

Waiting requires patience. It becomes an asset whereby as you wait, you are also seeking a higher calling, a divine intervention in your life.

Waiting should produce wisdom, knowledge, and understanding in our lives.
As you wait on God for your dreams and aspirations, will you trust that He can fulfill all that you think or image? (Ephesians 3:20)

Chapter Eight

Mentoring

> Then the LORD said to Cain, "Where is your brother Abel?" "I don't know," he replied. "Am I my brother's Keeper?" (Gen. 4:9, NIV)

You cannot say enough about the importance of mentoring, whether you are the recipient or the one who is providing mentoring. What a marvelous demonstration of what life is all about. Actually, it does not matter because the mentoring relationship is paid in full with many more blessings in return for both and the learning experiences that money cannot buy.

Most successful people would tell you that somebody took the time out of his or her busy schedule to give back to them, and this was what helped them on their journey.

Mentors help you avoid some of the pitfalls in life, and they help guide you through the rough terrain and valleys as you pursue your goals and dreams in life.

If you do not have a mentor, look around in your community and pray to God to lead you to someone whom you can trust, learn from; and also at the same time, you can give back to this individual for sharing with you. Once you have been mentored, it is expected that you will become a mentor and pass on knowledge, wisdom in your chosen field.

Chapter Nine

Thanksgiving

> Don't worry about anything; instead, pray about everything. Tell God what you need, and thank
> him for all he has done. (Phil. 4:6, NLT)

If you were raised with any type of manners, someone taught you to say "Thank you" when someone gives you something or shows kindness to you. It does not cost anything to tell the person thanks for his or her help. People will appreciate you more when you can show your gratitude and will more likely be willing to help you further advance your causes. A simple thank-you note can make the difference between favor or failure. Have you sent a thank-you note immediately after a job interview or after a college recruitment interview? **A little thank-you note can be your competitive edge over the competition and not just a good thing to do.**

In addition, being thankful is an expression of God's love and appreciation in your life. I believe if you were to make a list of all the experiences you have had in your lifetime, you would find that the good things in your life outweighed the bad or negative experiences in your life. Whom have you failed to say thank you to? It is never too late to express your thanksgiving to this person.

Chapter Ten

Celebrating

Mary responded, "Oh, how I praise the Lord. How I rejoice in God my Savior! For he took notice of his lowly servant girl, and now generation after generation will call me blessed." (Luke 1:46–48, NLT)

When you believe in yourself, trust and accept others for who they are, and submit to God so that His will be done in your life, I believe it is time to celebrate. You have reason to celebrate even if today is not your birthday or if you are still working hard on the job for that promotion or if you had a so-called bad day, week, month, or even year. The celebration that I am speaking of starts first within one's self, having the realization that he or she is better off today than yesterday and has come a long way in terms of thinking and growing to a higher level. In fact, each day brings you closer to achieving your goals. This is a cause for a celebration because you can now appreciate the lesser things in life as you have learned to live without them, sacrificed and worked very hard toward your goals in life step-by-step.

A celebration can break out when you are able to embrace others' differences in your family and community. It is okay that you are different or unique. You still are made in God's image, and He is proud of his beloved daughters and sons and expects us to share our gifts and talents with others.

What can you celebrate today in your life? Whom can you celebrate with after having gone through a great battle in life?

Chapter Eleven

Success

> This book of the law shall not depart out of thy mouth; but thou shalt meditate therein day and night, that thou mayest observe to do according to all that is written therein: for then thou shalt make thy way prosperous, and then thou shalt have good success. (Josh. 1:8, KJV)

Everyone is seeking to become successful in life. No one will tell you that he or she hopes to become a loser in life and hopes to fail at everything he or she does in life. If you were to ask someone who inspires him or her, names of successful people such as the late King of Pop Michael Jackson, Oprah Winfrey, Michael Jordan, President Barack Obama, and Michelle Obama would come to mind, just to name a few.

How would you measure success? Would you be able to recognize and appreciate someone who has worked hard and long hours to achieve a level of success? What are you willing to sacrifice right now?

Success means different things to different people. One person may say that he or she is successful if he or she can survive each day without getting shot in the dangerous streets of America or not becoming a statistic, finding himself or herself one of the two million persons incarcerated in the United States of America. Another may say that he or she is successful when he or she owns his or her business and makes his or her first one million dollars. Yet to another person, success is being able to see one's children grow up and live on their own. Someone may declare that he or she is successful when he or she is able to foster a child who was removed from his or her home due to abuse or neglect. Yet another person may say that he or she is successful if he or she can purchase his or her own home and live out his or her dreams. Some might question if it is still possible to live the American dream. Another person may declare that he or she is successful because he or she has learned that life is too short, and we must redeem the time each day and live each day with dignity, honesty and forgiving others who misuse or misunderstand us.

Sometime ago when I attended graduate school at the University of Connecticut working on a master of social work degree with a minor in community organization, in one of my papers, I defined success as this:

> Success is truly and wholeheartedly realized when the gaps are bridged so that all persons in the community can share in the prosperity, benefits and opportunities that life has to offer and bestow on all of humanity great and small.

However you view success in your life, do you agree on the following notions? (1) There are different definitions and meanings of success, (2) achieving success is a process and journey, and (3) there are different levels of success. I believe that if you are successful, it was meant for you to share with others and give back to those less fortunate than yourself.

Conclusion

For I know the plans I have for you, declares the LORD, plans to prosper you and not to harm you, plans to give you hope and a future. (Jer. 29:11, NIV)

With this in mind, we constantly pray for you, that our God may count you worthy of his calling, and that by his power he may fulfill every good purpose of yours and every act prompted by your faith. (2 Thess. 1:11, NIV)

Eleven essential components (purpose, excuses, forgiving, healing, networking, diligence, waiting, mentoring, thanksgiving, celebrating, and success) have been presented in this book to help you move toward living your dreams and purpose in life no matter what obstacles come in your life, and they will come. The Bible says in Psalms 23:4 that God will take you through the valley of the shadow of death; meaning, we will all have hardships in life, but God will take care of us, and we will be able to go through the valley and see green pasture on the other side if we don't give up and remain in the race.

Remember, each trial and test builds character; and all of our experiences, good and bad, are the grand total of who we are and all that we hope and pray to become in God's divine purpose for our lives!

Now you are ready to put the above principles into action by completing the exercises in the appendix, "Personal Development Growth Worksheet Exercise."

Appendix

PERSONAL DEVELOPMENT GROWTH WORKSHEET EXERCISE[1]

This worksheet was designed to help you identify areas (focal areas or goals) in your life where you are seeking personal development and growth based on God's promises in His Holy Word. This exercise will help you to write down action steps for each of your focal areas along with a commitment statement and agreement, as well as a visual exercise in order for you to see until your goals are actualized. As your goals are realized or changed, feel free to update and revise as needed anytime during the year. Pray to God for His direction before completing this worksheet. Completing this worksheet does not guarantee success, and the author is not responsible for your outcomes.

   1. Focal areas. List one to three major areas in your life you would like to concentrate on this year—for example, career advancement, retirement, health, friendship/dating, marriage, budgeting, ministry, business/ownership, family, parenting, etc.
   Focal area number 1 _____
   Focal area number 2 _____
   Focal area number 3 _____

   2. Supporting scriptures from the Holy Bible. For each of the above focal areas, list one to three scriptures. Each day throughout the year, you should read the scriptures along with your focal areas and action steps. For example, if one of your focal areas is working on not worrying, you can look up in your Bible concordance scriptures that address worrying. Matthew 6:34 (NIV) states, "Therefore do not worry about tomorrow, for tomorrow will worry about itself. Each day has enough trouble of its own." In 1 Peter 5:7 (NIV), "Give all your worries and cares to God, for he cares about what happens to you." (It may be helpful to use index cards to write your scriptures on.)

---

1   Note: This worksheet was created by Winston Taylor, MSW, for his personal, professional, and spiritual growth before each New Year since 2007. All rights are reserved. Feedback and workshop bookings can be sent to winston_taylor@sbcglobal.net or by calling (860) 889-3292.

3. Action steps. For each focal area, list as many as needed action steps you would need to take in order to help realize your focal areas. For example, if you choose to improve your health, some of the action steps could include walking fifteen minutes each day, joining and going to the gym two to three times a week, eating healthier foods, cooking healthier foods, taking a class, or seeing a nutritionist, etc.

4. Commitment statement and agreement. On a separate paper, write a commitment statement to yourself, sign and date it.

5. Visual display/collage. Find pictures from magazines, words and objects that give you a visual picture of your above focal areas and post them on a cardboard surface or poster board and look at it every day.

Contact and Booking Information

E-mail: winston_taylor@sbcglobal.net

Telephone: (860) 889-3292